The Tower of Diverse Shores

by Leonard Schwartz

Poetry

Objects of Thought, Attempts at Speech (1990)
Exiles: Ends (1991)
Gnostic Blessing (1992)
Words Before The Articulate (1997)
The Tower of Diverse Shores (2003)

Essays

A Flicker At The Edge of Things:
Essays Towards A Poetics (1998).

Co-editor

Primary Trouble: An Anthology of
Contemporary American Poetry (1996)
An Anthology of New (American) Poets (1998)
Crossing Centuries:
The New Generation in Russian Poetry (2000)

Leonard Schwartz

The Tower of Diverse Shores

9/03
For Joe -
with many thanks
and with
pleasure - amazement -
in your work...
Best,
Leonard S

Talisman House, Publishers
Jersey City, New Jersey

Published in the United States of America by
Talisman House, Publishers
P.O. Box 3157
Jersey City, New Jersey 07303-3157

Manufactured in the United States of America
Printed on acid-free paper

Acknowledgments

Some of these poems first appeared in *American Letters & Commentary, Barrow Street, Colorado Review, Conjunctions, Cross Cultural Poetics, D.C. Poetry Anthology* 2002, *Fence, First Intensity, Gallerie Internationale* (India), *Jacket, New American Writing, Oficina De Poesia* (Portugal), *Poetry New York, Pool, Quarterly Review of Literature Singapore, Talisman, The Bard Papers, The World, Trace, Trepan, UrVox, Van Gogh's Ear, Verse* and *Vert. Thanks to the respective editors of these journals.*

CONTENTS

III

IV

The Tower of Diverse Shores

I

Craft

Circe is a certain kind of light.

Body, heavy with sleep, awakens sleek,
on the good side of that enchantress.

And everything again becomes strange.

So the current is animated
by other forces

An unseen rivulet in the river
revitalizing the river

Becoming the river
returned to itself.

So enshrined in arms of flesh and chests
of flesh, poured from earth's lips

Speech, as multiform and rapid
as the flight of pigeons.

Out of a lightness of ear
lifts the butterfly of skill.

By eyes grazed, grazing objects,
form is nudged from unconscious haunts.

All is sacred, one bridge to diverse shores.

Hudson Curve

Silence defects the grove
and the grove goes silent.

For fear of silence
all trees are slaughtered.

Then mingle the sea gulls
and the crows

As is only possible on a thin slip
of waterfront and grass.

And if I saw a hummingbird
it was no illusion.

And the red light associated with Mars
whose locus remains the intellect's shine,

The thinking part of the twinkle.
Nowhere shows the other god's name

But the hummingbird
must go somewhere to drink

And silence perches on the border
between idea and the next strata

Saws at work
trimming the sinecure.

Heard thunder, sought to include
unsuspected roses and Norwegian elm

Migration of forms
reverentially tended

Talents of thatch
to which Tu Fu retired.

No going back save for the river,
reversing its current routinely.

Circle Line they call the boat
brings the visitors

Around Manhattan Isle,
Circle Line.

Ecstatic Persistence

Continuous revelation of,
no subject but light.

Too, tied to the stake
    of foundational doubt.

Steam off rocks of this perception.

And snow monkeys. On their thrones.
Of stone. In the steam. Illuminated.

Action taken equals miracle.

Burning stake.

Or a world away:
a lament in tones so sweet the tones
permeate

This composition,
this drinking
establishment —

  no, never the establishment —

(we seek to inhabit
what cannot be inhabited)

Yet the eye emerges whole.

Outside in that world

The voice dances as through trees
and who moves is like the bird

Deigning to primogeniture
knowing dark bloods and eye-buds

A snow monkey giving birth in snow
a splash of red, perception fired

Where they eat the golden apples
and never get old and so forth

Figures on a stage
that lead miniature lives, zoo creatures
in the action of language

Wildness withheld, hope to uncover

The being outside the bars
at labor in the steam off those waters.

   Would ask the music for help.

Would listen till I was out of my head
only they'd rightly say

         escapist.

So when the song
      is sealed,

let variously dispersed elves

Congregate

Let the ale in a glass, amber in color,
be drunk

And be replaced with ale, equally amber

Equally amber

Until the snow monkey

until the snow monkey

until the snow monkey.

Divided Silence

Experiment warms you like a rose;
the great circus sprinkles you with dust
the self can neither pick over nor wall off.

And the philosopher is charged with a divided silence.

Like a gray wall he empties himself
of all wild meaning, turned two-tongued by his project.

Manmade as the language of these men
you juggle the journals of actual prophets.

The great circus sprinkles you with dust
and the comet adjusts to its new population.

Experiment warms you like a rose.

Wrong Track

In your translation
the "bird's twitter" read
"a twig's snap."

I translated "the chirp of the cicada"
as "the chirp of the cicada" —

But that was wrong.

I'm sorry
I couldn't hear you

I'm sorry
but the principle of habit is the principal habit

The literal translation of "habit" is "mountain"
I'd entered my Himalayas without bringing my chimes.

Gift

The world tries to be beautiful
but the blindness part breaks in

And that's me, my looking away.
So doubt slices through the principle thing:

We're no better off than before doubt.
Neither are the roses perceived on the counter
          just then.

The Total Work of Art

Mirrors capture in their glass
the lush, saliva-flecked mirth of the singer.
But from the circus of her very real exertions
only a cassette drops out, months later.

Just so what Thought once hedged to call the All
is today regarded as the dreamless hum of the global —
except for certain peels of life, forever floating.
Think how your exhalations still build worlds.

And the phone booth — who dares to step in there?
Only one who is human flesh and still sips wine,
yet is born to the number he's going to dial. Sometimes
the rhetorically darker aria affords the greater warmth.

The Frown

Comes the daybreak that does not ask to be buttoned up
but leaves its shoulders bare.
The fathers don't approve of that
but in any case naked forms are what they love to see.

It's what they've bred. Yet they've never married,
the tall egret just happened. They'd been off fishing
and in the aftersmoke, colorful and heavily oiled,
something raised its head, and laughed, and scarcely needed

Further advice. Yet they pester it
with made up dreams. They confer teeth upon the bee.
With its extra bones the bee flies all heavy to a woman
and is a woodpecker lodged faintly in her leg.

Lyric

A single nail head holds it.

Bees are its vocabulary.

A lion swats at it
through the transcribed hum.

Neither splintered,
for finally it is won.

Such lyric, as it's welded, is not sturdy,
even to the singer is indistinct —

No god grafts the earth to our feet
and should His sunshine penetrate these vocal chords

We'd study
how to unstud that proffered phlegm

Lyric a delighted clarity
not for clergymen.

Knowledge in the nail.
Explicit want.

A *single* nail head holds it.

Poem To Morpheus

1. Plea

Light-footed agent,
help slow me down.
My invocation to you alone,
Master Morpheus,
you alone can aid me.
Its you that grant
the limb relaxing rest.
Its you who steep
the mind in springs
bring the mind to rise
alert. When speech melts
into the bad infinite, a monologue:
when the dark is lit with gall:
when the brain is bees:
you alone can end it.
Morpheus, guide my breath.
I promise you more poems.
I promise you more poems
when I am fresh.

2.

Temple
that for a single statuette
is indistinguishable from
a narrow cot:

Morning sings the name of Morpheus!

Delight in the mind's leap to consciousness,
      to a design,
hallowed by the mystery
of a good night's sleep,
of looking back to it in thanks
beneath a concert of bells gone crazy.

After just a single draught from that deep aquifer,
      the light brings bushes,
a curving belly mounted by cypress breasts,
the meadow to which my guide now leads me.

Again, Morpheus,
my deepest thanks.

Elations

1

Bitter cold prostitute
and Romanian hero, lover and father-in-law.
It's slate gray sky or love on the terrace,
its avenues of water or a walk in the slums.

Home. Also home. Ruined houses. A friend's
extra cot. Out to the biergarten. In her parent's
bed. All alone under the Pantheon's dome. The crowd
at the ruins. The crowd on the ferry.
Awaiting transport to a coastal town.

2

On a colossal scale
   and then there was glass.
An iron Lenin bereft on the square.
Streets that were quiet now owned by the car.
Jones Beach, radio free: silent bonanza.
Strolled through the tropical town.
Air as heavy as standing water.
Rainstorm after rainstorm
during the lightest of sleeps.
The temple and its ancient trees
thirsting for a breeze.
Sweeping in early in the morning, glad
      to find a bed.

Glad to find
    her in the bed:
sunbathers naked in the *Englishgarten.*
Jumped through a wave, tasted the sea.
The pickpocket's white hand
slipped right past my cock.
Next:
to meet Thomas at the TransAmerica at 2AM.

3

Leaning at ease
against Suleiman's wall,
grapes in one hand
Rimbaud in the other
(was eighteen years old).
In a dark glade Mayakovsky's grave
only last summer.
Went out for a short walk:
seventy year old and seven year old
scouring the streets.
Returning to Kennedy, disguised as the person
who had previously left.
Rome's swallows reminded her
of Beijing summer,
the same hungry sound.
Harmonious hut:
chorus of birds around five in the morning.
Stretched out in the field far from the town.
A plaque to honor Endre Ady, Hungarian poet;
Lucacs, translated into French, browsed on the train.

4

Days in the souks,
out of this world.
Withdrawn behind the icons.
Barefoot on the Lady Dowager's grounds
and the other man, deep in thought.
Cioran introduced me to the Italian editor
but she wasn't interested.
Asked if I'm Islamic
like Muhammad Ali, told to get off the bus
and never look back.
Grapes in one hand, Rimbaud in the other,
evidently attractive: a gay Arab
from Hebron making his play.
Out on the piers with Marina and Ulf:
    holding Ulf's hand.
Out on the piers with Jaime and Indran:
    held hands with Mingxia.
Out on the piers with Yang Lian and Yo Yo:
    they didn't touch.
Downpour on Jane Street,
    no point to clothes.
An exquisite black cat: Jerusalem *chi.*
A shack on stilts at the edge of the sea.

5

"John Street,
what a suggestive name,"
the woman said dryly,

out in the drizzle in a
drab yellow skirt.
E.W. too down in the dumps —
a turtle in a trench coat
miserable in the turbid rain.
Old lady vending a single garment
in the Mayokovskaya metro corridor;
an even more elderly lady hawking
    Siberian kittens.
Pregnant British woman glimpsed in her tub,
heard she'd died seven years later:
meeting her daughter along Avenue Daumesnil.
Dead cat, burned up, stashed in an urn.
Love meets bad luck on certain
of these turns, love meets a roadside
resurrection in the old quarter
of mysteriously selected towns, not failing
to mention the city is divided in spirit
between haves and have nots.

6

Locked in the garden at Versailles
after closing hours we slowly undressed
for the camera (I only saw the photographs once).
She knew a wall she wanted us to sit on;
when we sat, we were spellbound by the fading Etruscan sun.
Staten Island cab drivers, many from Ghana;
the ones I meet, I ask about Gassire.
"How much did you see of conspicuous consumption?"
    SK queries after the trip.

In ignorance of muezzin
writing out passages from Artaud
at 2 in the morning: chills through my spine
as the call to prayer sounds, sensual loudspeakers
electrifying the transcribed mummy named in the text.
The grasslands stretched before us.
Knew no one in the city and liked it that way,
lived each day in expectation of the next sun,
the clouds of unknowing it was sure to condense.
They go out of their way to make it look artsy,
twisting the room in the manner of glass
and leaving you with precious little space to get passed,
a kind of revenge of the culture against its practitioners,
unless you like that kind of closed-in feeling, and some do.
"The elderly here look older than the elderly
seen anywhere else," his first letter said, and his last.
Bitterness pervades my memory of that city:
  I cannot say why.
Brought her back from the airport
and into the shower, clothing and all.
Afterwards we looked bowlegged from riding
the horses, svelte and unsaddled,
so far from the yurts.

7

Hudson Street under the hammer,
the same bearded waiter, year after year.
Small room in a great lodge, made it that far.
Mists rising out of valleys and over trees
the lumber industry mercifully spares.

Marble Hill: spotted an egret.
Flew into Rio, egrets at attention
in acrid pools encircling the airport.
Snowswept cityscape either side of the Wall.
Shubinsky gesticulated in a stiff awkward way.
The Valley of Fex, cow blocking our path.
Tel Aviv dive, too terrifying to fathom.
Fountain in the Luxembourg Garden
around which Celan paced as he mumbled
in his very last years.
Hutong she grew up in, familiar, unfamiliar
    ramble and twist.
Jersey Turnpike and surrounding murk also
inhabited by egrets, on the way to work
glimpsed as they fish.

8

Fulton Street Fish Market
after the storm, dead fish and live turtles
plastering Water Street.
Gawking down Gorki's steps
two giant salamanders, their mouths fixed
in a smile, made of green stone apparently soft.
Meltingly soft sun near the *Theatre du Soleil,*
sordid recollections of Tenderloin raunch.
The turtle crept forward on uncertain feet.
Arrived at the Haitian joint for New Year's Eve
very much late, danced away what was left of our time.
Confederate flag flying over Miami Beach
construction site; B- for the A train.

Sat in the Chekkov Center not understanding a word.
A city I like but cannot see detail in.
From Paris to Dieppe everything a blur.
C+ for the A train, C- for the 1.
Advertisement for a strip-club
dangled from an airplane:
shuffling past the embalmed leader
too slowly for the guards.
Awaiting the hurricane with windows shuttered;
that storm never happened, NYC's did.
Enjoyed existence, took a dip in the Wadi.
A for the A train equals being-in-itself.
Being as movement equals the action of change.

9

"Fafner" deep in sleep at Lincoln Center?
The snake bit but not through the boot.
Ghostly march up many steps
to reach the women's section
and the canoe began to drift.
Wotan, unsure which way to turn,
settles on the Heights.
Aging gracefully, Scandanavian cruise.
Darkened synagogue of spiraling ascents.
Jonah as translated for comic effect:
"are you angry?" the prophet queries
his divinity figure, the counter-will's face.
Pacing the room as the younger man frothed,
from the smoothness of stones to the Ligurian sea.
Wore the yarmulke to decontextualize his head.

Climbing the switchbacks without a place to stay.
Night falls on the forest;
drinking a beer at the inn *Elefante*.
Chirp of insects, supernaturally bright stars.
To begin to distinguish differences where everything
in the city seemed uniformly drab?
It took about 72 hours in the offing.
Later, the song of the birds, its sense, their
whereabouts, an unfathomable source.

The Blue Jay

Certain silences to be honored,
other silences that ought to be defied.
The sinister ringmaster hid the big jeweled box
holding distinction, kicked the clown
who dared approach the center ring.
And all continued as if nothing had happened.
Perhaps the smiling impresario sprinkled
more Amazon creation myths into his patter,
held up the Orinoco Basin as his juggler's goal.
And it was as if the heads of two rivers were mingling,
turbulent and muddy, disrespectful of each other's zones,
happy to prove there was something to be said
but it should never be uttered.

Motionless between these two readings
a boulder thrust forward near the confluence's lip.
About this boulder nothing can be said. Besides,
the juggler already advanced to the bit with torches.
And as soon as the audience turned its back
the blue jay broke for the egg it had coveted.
Thieves are always that way, breaking into birthplaces
or violating the sacred tombs of the dead.
Then the ringmaster turned everyone's attention to Virgil,
the point in the story where the past river
and the river of the future finally converge.
Steal in for a dip. These waters are silent.

Sonnet

Something obscure throbs in my love.
Make-believe bed, blanket and belly,
opened pores . . . All this baffles
the adamant tongue . . . I signal I'm ready . . .
mirrors and earth fall from my grip.

It comes from the heat.
How else would summer store sadness?
Fondle with surprise the leaves in the gutter.
This snatching at, this fucking
that once in awhile is solemnly elevated

And clearly combusts,
double-cognized, quivering
omniscient ravenous arch-alcohol
aching to bite what you don't recall.

Cigar with Sherry

Ask me amid the exultant shouts
what I am seeing, and I will shout back:

"I do not know.
It cannot be seen."

Orbs reimagine greater orbs,
and bland becomes sweet

Out of nowhere arises
there is no precedent.

It is a season in which glass melts, doors unhinge,
not from any heat — it is all in the hearing —

But from the disappearance of grounds
for any separation from oneself.

Even vegetation takes on new feeling.
Liquid in the air, as warm as living blood

Circulates over floating lawns.
The sound of a cat licking its fur

Then other harmonies, those that do not
name for you their source.

So that the old way of being no longer pertains
to the rippling of these sensoriums

Lips, lungs, ears
all participants in some unspoken breaking point.

Not a dream, this soft moaning
around the perimeters of the ozone.

Nor is it the obvious apocalypse that is happening
for the living still cling to the living

The wail of the siren in the street announces.
The mind so rarely parts with custom —

Spring, summer, winter, fall —
yet something is changing in the way

The head does its drinking,
in the atmosphere dreaming makes for itself.

This new and undefined season . . .
this euphoria of retraction . . .

Horn Dwelling

In far wilderness yonder toothy bard
engages in commerce with a discharged heaven.
Sings of arcane lizards, slender backwoods
encircling detected and undetected peaks.
The leftover rice? Your portion is beside
the bush, by the dry anthill of the Ancient's tomb.
Dense thickets thieve the arrows there,
leave you holding charcoal chunks;
but the meadow beyond is as white as a cat.
Hurry off, then, to those lofty grasses glorying
in soft wet soil. All the parts are moving.
Each thistle, every rarity, is refreshed by a nap.

II

Difficult Passage

Though it corresponds with X, the portrait is already changing,
in a direction that was pointedly authorized well before,
when any of us were sovereign over what now is sublimated
    once, when thought was time.
And whenever this kind of undertow exacts itself,
there are many scenes played back for further clarification,
and the being of being-perceived is re-enacted,
this time from the inside of its rectangular shell.

Any point on such a time-line can be represented,
only this one point is not
neither X, nor not-X.
Yet detached from the official portrait
it can provide only a Xerox of the past.
Like the dope wagon hooked onto the rest of the train,
fusing imperceptibly with everything heading in the one direction.
Or the Coke bottle, an emblem of the American way of life,
propagated in popular advertising all over the world,
filling with liquid from some other space.
This is the point at which a mattress rises from the surf,
  responsive to all signifiers.
It too is American.

Mostly there are minds that wake up in the morning
ready for action and untroubled by waves.
They say, "no choice but the one that pretends there is choice"—
a truth that does not hold for *Difficult Passage*.
In fact, nothing holds less at the margin of time.
Drop by drop it is the dismemberment of water

the lifting of foam
        section of the portrait. This is where we are,
this is it, now this. While we cannot summon
the coordinates of these our correspondences
the red dust on the floor boards shines more brightly
when the sun is finally centered.

Camargue

You who endow me
with eel, I want to taste you
who conditions like the wind,
speaks in the watercourse.

Disseminated among reeds, you run
as a marshland runs, slowly.
Knees like fishing beds I wade in worship.
Deliberate as sea lavender against calf.

Yet nothing is outward in you, not even
driving rain, loosening the lagoon's
buried relics, preparing the next sediment
as potsherds wash up beside long flamingo dresses.

Whence the light undergoes — submersion.
Which will make a murky subject in that half-world
flocking so seasonally into this field where I am dying.
How will I who am not alluvial layer myself?

I will go to the beach. I will offer myself
as earthenware, in emanation you will be a leaf.
One is the clay, one goes on yielding.
Inside the newly assumed shell I quiver at the beak.

Waterway

for Gustaf Sobin

Plunged into that lagoonal grail
of which he had been speaking as if forever.

Knee deep in nutrients the knowledge
    that all is water:
what could never be solid ground
is the only ground, miasma of the mind
the mind is when itself,
pronouns on red alert for a murky god
or marsh rabbit quick to swim at snap of twig.

If logs float silently over sleep's ferment
then turtles bask on logs lodged in sunshine,
    all available pronouns lost in that lagoonal grail
each day visited by a repeating structure,
variants of a haunted grammar
at once irritated and impearled.

It's a waterway older than the wheel,
yet never twice, never twice the same wetness of things.
No fountain of youth, only a fountain of fish
ospreys lift from slough to sky.

Dynamic Ensemble

for Gustaf Sobin

A fractured aqueduct still conducts a limpid charge.

He dreamt of frescoe angels
of an anti-faith.
Infant orange supplant agent orange,
please: peach
so pleases
the hands that receive it.

And an almost involuntary smile,
the product of joy in a particular presence:
    joy peels
from the near-rhyme
/so much for the scythe/.

Rippling sound of water flowing.

Comfort repeatedly touches Hurt,
some lucid source
in brooks and stones,
the interior's coiled life,
as the wind that removes a plaything
may return it.

I'm what's hummed by Reticence and Desire.
    In any event
I'm painting my own light
— it's not mine at all —

in which solid and fluid are one
as rain falls in the fluvial parts.

It's a supersensitivity which is its own great power,
a palpable, almost visible energy,
emotion that pours
from a lip region mistaken
for the physical.

A fractured aqueduct still conducts a limpid charge.

Trickle

As freshwater
dreams itself into salt water.

To speak, to speak into the wound of listening,
into the hesitation of gardens on the verge
of the willingness to grow,
these reassuring undulations released in the sub-soil.

The thermoluminescent moment gaped blonde.

What moves you moves me; I'm moved.

Opaque mirrors — our hearts
serpentine — adored the new sun.

Finally, to live in the dazzle

in its most flexible chambers of abundance,
as moisture collects in those delicate tidal pools,
  a flower at the core of the sea.

It's the world beginning and the world coming to an end,
and our knowing only the beginning, ever the beginning.

It's a question of the body's natural resins.

Lines for Aeschylus

A woman holds a time capsule
and inside the net Agamemnon is crying.

A man and a woman are dwarfed by their own home
and inside a bed room closet
their son discovers a terrible daylight.

Inside an inward part vulcanized
thirty-three years ago

Prophets were wombed. So was pounding rain.
Honey rose from a vulviform cup.

The Furies are in the honey.

Achilles' Song

My life at odds with itself,
my flags at half-mast for myself
Find myself weeping at the shore
a rage rougher than rip-tides
Pent up in my vanquished cells:

Mother, dearest goddess, how dare they
do me this dishonor, disgrace *Achilles*
I'd pound the pounding surf
    but what's the point
Now my limbs unfurl
like those of the dust eaters
just yesterday I dispatched.

My friends are my opponents,
    my friends are many
And my opponents are my bane
From this hour forward I build a refusal
to advance to recognize to feel
Yes, I'll build my blood right into the coral
hair and sea weed, you make the perfect match.

Dearest Goddess
bury all my opponents, one by one
in scores to feed my rage, o please

Heaving gray sea, be my blanket.

Reader In Extremis

The poem tells of gargantuan fame,
boasts made on ancient ramparts,
loss that multiplied with the passage of each dawn.

Look: a soldier scans the gathering clouds,
his face reflecting dead companions.

A wind has been commanded to churn the surf :
  like children out of control
The breakers it creates leave nothing standing.

And just as the fighting of the past will some day
foray into the present, a ton of heartbreak
  as certain as the knot of sex,
so just now a mouth can taste ambrosia:

You have loved,
and keep an ear to the thundering sky

You have loved,
and scan the surface of the foaming lanes

Not wanting to tear yourself away
something temporary so soon become a citadel

As though where you were was plunder
  worth lingering over,
And, deep in attachment, you could break the pattern.

Orgasm Sonnet

Charon, I'm not a passenger on this ride,
just a pilgrim. Inside your barque,
drenching space to make possible
parables germinate, that's one thought.
And every one of us who raves
wants another such thought to follow.

I know your bosses would prefer to render
all of us blank. So what? Even now
we're filling your ferry with come.
So that, exhausted by our planet's
unbreakable desire, when it comes
time to try to tinfoil me on the other side
you'll only find my anonymous likeness:
I'll have already really died.

Pages From An Imaginary Escape

Festooned abstraction
        the bridge mirrors the mind.

To leap from there to sky

flooded with sun beams,
girders, air space

"permanently" gulping "instantly,"
"instantly" gulping "permanently"

Then what of the bridge?

Brigge, brugge, log, beam, stick
hence wooden causeway
to provide a way across

Tightly strung web tensed in the haze

between elevated observer
and pedestrian palisade

The strings of an instrument tingling to be touched

Each flare of perception
a lonely peregrination
of the formless into form

A fulgurating synthesis
arched over a rush of broken bones

*

Pour of traffic,
 a river over a river under a stream.

Beam: to give out shafts of light
and *baum,* a tree.

Pore: originally a passage, a channel.

As in the unbearable moment in which the eye
seeks out something excluded from the scene

Then dislodged from its socket
is flung into the froth

The goddess known as "active tongue,"
 as "ravenous mouth"

Smoothly takes
all things ripe and heavy
in her hands,

Barely perspiring
guides them
to her namesake.

Still enveloped,
 like fruit sucked by its own skin,
these self-same things
 tremble before the altar.

O sun whore
destroy this field

of pores —
hold my health in your mouth
and I will pay for it in words

finger the imagination's furnace
    palus a stake
or the fate of the palisade at stake

demand I flood you
            holy harlot
and I'll forget my name

at the top of the tower
where water wets the seeds

a language made to
rise from the language
like sap

engorged glades of river life
wave their sticky heads
as if on spindles

blue sky, white clouds
the sun aglow
with the semen
it has sucked

fellatio to
festival
to *perpetual feast*

makes up a world where there is none

✲

Mist wound tight
around the portal

each phoneme
at play for me

to imagine anew
a reference

its assigned/unassigned
think now of a tugboat plowing upriver

and a theory of imagination
that predates both the perception

and the river

a theory is a fruit
a fear and a binding

a boat moves up a river
at biblical speed

An auditory replaces an ocular vocabulary
and the mind leaves off its mirroring.

As for the need of a transition:

Beneath the muffled engines of the commuter caravan
beneath the black chirps of the cicadas

if you listen with greater care

An armada of other worlds sails
into your quarantine in the here and now

At the edge of indeterminacy
someone has recently revived galleons

Firing cannons at the here and now

Prideful vessels that transport
sunlight from one lifetime into the next.

Or else two shores
at either end of an evidential gap

Rain falling
on the apparition of a bridge

From the topmost leaves
the drops run off

As an invisible foghorn sounds —
when this run off and that foghorn are one

Comes an instant of "gradually"
soothing the senses —

Airy abstraction that bursts
into moisture and tone —

Is not lost in the ancient world
   time as a structure of beauty.

* *

The remedy for my bouts with suffocation:
the wind as it rattles the air
at altitudes above the encampment

Blue mirror, perforated veil

heart as sudden as a train-whistle

in a prior space of contemplation
where, to exaggerate, objects are so rarefied
they are not there if you aren't.

How odd, that when the architecture is dwarfed
          the mind goes free

But that can only happen
from the tops of other edifices

Building giving distance to building
in a supersession of views.

To insist *in all this labor*
      only ourselves
deprives the making of its mystery

and yet I admit

the tale *is* entirely human in its sailing,
a vessel of light anchorless and aglow
   in the already engineered

A porthole looking out
over our own estrangement

A map of projections in a book
beside other printed matter.

But such is also an ideal
of rising joy, the transport
of a figurative sustenance

Next to which the natural and the divine
are seen as a telling out of one

Auto-intoxication, auto-immolation,
   automobiles, bumper to bumper
on the bridgeway below

"A felt architectonics then
              of the numinous"

Pictured and unpictured thought

Loft of vision, telepathy of wires

Patience its antithesis, the infirmity of conviction.

The Washington Bridge, completed October 25th, 1931:
The great cable towers of the bridge rise 335 feet into the air, two and a third times as high as those of the Brooklyn Bridge. Thus in 50 years the physical scale of engineering has more than doubled itself, as may be seen also in the relative length of the main river spans of the two bridges, 3500 and 1600 feet.

A nightly drilling into rock and lichen:

through labor
the instant is worked
into the repository
of "was," "is," and "will be"

in leisure this grid holds

beyond labor and leisure
there is no time.

Capitalism and its accretions:

a dream of knowledge
that presumes a verifiable future

an act of perception
that takes as its tactics the here and now

the suck of experience
that draws us towards a pre-established past

beyond these
no one dares speak —

the promised eternal doubling —

lest articles of faith founder on the edge of lore.

A transcript of what happened Somewhere Else
Above all, that is the time that must be spoken with
Against the wishes of the demiurge
That creative being who sings like the Sirens
An apt metaphor for God.
North American Rapture on the dole
By dint of advertisement's kill of language.
Awaken from your shipwreck!
Bright light and swamped canoe,
Global gods and goddesses that used to clash
Believing falsely they could not die,
Tomorrow's sky chopped into quadrants:
All forms are fragile when countered by force
Force a form too but not the first.
Pore: originally a passage, a channel, a tiny mouth
Limbs refracted into ribs and cables.
Not the energy behind all commerce and consumption
Not the right to shop at Shop Rite
Or to rend one another limb from limb
But the American knowledge that all that rises
Arose so recently
There once was another time
A spiritual principle to be applied to the present
Without romanticism —
To wit,
To go forward into the betterment.

✡

Achilles bestride the cliffs
forgotten his human side
ear turned from the sea —
divine without knowledge of the source
Thetis as hidden as a pearl
to the rage of his projections.

Violence regales the sky,
the sea, both shores;
sharks teeth glimmer
on the river's waves.
To kill — what?
The world sacrifices itself
to its own image.

"The orchestration of sun and sight
has been other on every morning
since reaching the newly discovered land" —
words attributed to an early explorer
    previously undiscussed

let us call him Vasco Pajama.

"The seagulls are larger and more white
than the seagulls at home,
the waterways more wet.
I think we have reached some great pleroma."

"Perhaps if we continue inland some more years
    all we've left behind will seem imaginary
and these surroundings our norms"
   continues Pajama
in a late log entry
just before bedding down.

But the next morning he returns
to the earlier trope:

"the unknowns always outweigh the knowns"
  and
"So what if in my sleep I no longer see the womb?
New territory is also an interior unfolding."

In fainter script:

"For my log alone:
I have worn the mask of greed

only to please Queen and crew,
or any — of what I view.
May no one ever follow my lead into these parts
for with the crowd comes thirst for goods and God,
  the failure of my perfect escape.
Let everything here remain strange and I the stranger.
To be disoriented is to be filled with love."

Soon after this the Pajama party
disappeared into the sleepless void.

Pajama had discovered America.

Clytemnestra bestride the metropolis
that in all its formal rectitude and size
resembles Agamemnon writhing in his net —
accursed house of mastery, enslavement, and slaughter
the coast of this or any other North American town.

Revenge does not so much befoul as bequeath
its progenitor a cause and effect no one kept in mind.
Orestes unborn(not seen), Orestes in exile(not seen),
Orestes standing over his murdered mother,
a mouth to suck his hands of self-renewing blood
Yes, here are the snapshots in the family
tabloid, the ones we've developed. And Justice?
Athena, jury, they do not convince
or relieve the mind of the hot flash of injustice
just as an end does not conclude
but only marks a new beginning —
Not in absolution or punishment carried out pro forma
can the accursed cycle leave off from murder
but only by the construction of a negative time and place
unforeseen archipelagos in the hindmost stars
a considered staging   a veiled intoxication
beyond the pages of an aborted escape
and the slaveship's stinking holds.

III

Point of Entry I

Certain portals, happily, just hang around:
    closed, they're open:
hinged but limpid
their surfaces teem with engravings.

Yet one lusts for a material language.
Air as still as a sad suitor
who inwardly, alas, oscillates
before such portal, in the swollen interval of doubt.
Who sees none of those fluid but inalterable forms
    spawned just there, swimming outwards.

Is it the Queen of Thought that is
maladroit, or are those your own rough renderings?
Mood caws, swift to project a wall.
A crow as black as tea leaves, but
it's with hot tea that nature kneels to human action,
cups of porcelain fill with running life —
in which each ripple of light opens a door.

Like that sitting rock I'd rejoiced over.
Or that moist sapling delicately anchored
    on the far-off hill.

And when it comes time to name
those manifold willows whose frail bodies
each weep differently, for a different sun,
all immense beneath the creeping curtain of fire,

Then from the marvelous river-banks
lifts a single silken bridge.

A white moth, this evening's motif, hunts its mate
through orientalized labryinths of lace.

There

In the annals of the sun this day was sunny,
in the records of the moon this night was full.
And in the tides account of today's highs and lows
its agendas were met precisely.

You wandered through it, you were there.
If that doesn't count, that doesn't count
   but that won't be your fault.
Fortunate the words that fall on the sand.

Far Away, June

From palms you learned care,
from poplars reverie:

always on your way into unknown parts,
behaving as if the seasons
were filled with boundless milk, possibly heated.

The latest teaching's tar may harden:
you'll never be more than bodies joining
        just off the road.

It's the stunted spruce, the American journey.

Ogling holiness one's likely to get ordained
while the true orgy is going on in an open hut.

If it comes, it comes.

Meanwhile whatever it is makes sorrow adhere
        to Formica kitchen counters
is listed in easily ordered manuals of previous longing.

Just twist the cap and by liquid's end
        you're perfectly stunned.

Taste these cherries, pass them on:
they'll help you passionately mount.

Eight Glimpses of Earth

for Tan Dun

1

The landscape can only be approached by means of what is empty in oneself. I enter it by the headlights of content, then subtract everything from my surroundings that appears to have been illuminated. I know of no other way out of the pretense involved in the very act of looking. Difficult, isn't it, separating out the countryside from the service door you wish to enter?

2

The senses almost echoing in their abandon, it's limitless this calling between the pages and maybe experiencing something.

But without the persistent desire to lift words from the tumult of coincidence, to tinker by voice with minor happening after minor happening, a certain melting pot of things would never be set to music, there would be nothing to call into.

Hence the attraction of setting out to recuperate old visions, of selecting from orbs of one's own persistent translation, reanimating the senses, establishing unavoidable differences of meaning at decent enough intervals, like pylons, until, in this way, along this route and this route alone, the regimented views of the censorial apparatus at last become outdated, and not in the wavering lines of those old visions.

3

Yes, even the order to begin to censor a certain hope or feeling must be written down. And yes, even that order can get "lost in the translation." And as it bleeds itself (a form of circulation), it changes, becomes its other, coagulates to break apart, is forgotten as such and remembered elsewhere, until instead of a general principle or categorical command, the enigma of a personal project proclaims its solo dance. That's language, like a bongo. With the desire ending up expressed anyway, a kind of rhythm without melody, a way of looking into the air while listening to ceramic instruments specifically designed for the purpose. "Eat, drink, there is plenty," a hardy voice announces. But that too can be conceived of as an "exile," can't it — an "almost" that in the cloudy soup I cannot see or taste, that scalds by association and only refers to flavor indirectly, where original and parody are all-communicating, almost complementary — I won't say it — ingredients of the broth?

4

Wet tiles, blue vines printed on the shower curtain. And outside the curtain? Somehow I've lost my way among my hoary effigies and cumbersome shadows and druids of eld, awoken under the scalpel of some plastic surgeon of the forest. Maybe it was last night's shuffling of maps which led to my later being misled along an old Indian trail of in-jokes — and I not in the in. Like hugging at high speed to the curves of a highway in the passes, festive with the ceremonies of nature — then finding out you don't have any nature.

When one is beautiful it is hard to understand this.

5

A living chunk is placed on display, an explanatory card to it side reading "this is mere association." Nothing here is merely association. The earth does not associate, she brings together, insists these pieces join, no matter how unlike in composition. Look at the geologies she arrives at, from so many parts — a living chunk of it is now on display. But a forest will soon grow over it. On the trail will be found some eavesdroppings — fresh, still steaming — and those searching will know the eaves could not be far ahead. They will ready their weapons and stand, listening. Sensitive to the slightest snapping of a twig. But they will not hear a thing.

6

Downtown at full moon, a fundamental pitch is produced, from jars and ceramics come resonating earth sounds, a music that presents to us the stoneware of our thought, cleansed of abstract posture. And the instrumentalists who perform it are only a beach on which the sonorities break, a human support for the earth in all its signaling, reality revivified as it passes through some animal skins. For seconds, to live in the bass chants of this performance, come near the silken strings. Something ancient and yet not the same as an echo of the past. Unceasingly active in its inversions. At all times a sort of pure beginning. *Ritual without referent is precisely the goal.*

7

I have tasted of the *pharmakon* — that word which is both the remedy and the poison — and concluded that it need not have been drunk at all for us to have ended up addicted, sleepless, beaming with the bones of all prior form, giving of bone and flesh and blood to all the forms that had none. One ends up an addict by the simple act of breathing. Air is the true *pharmakon,* earth its container.

8

The earth is that place in the rain
after redemption.   *After redemption?*
After the thought of you and I
entering it to be redeemed.   *Redeemed?*
By the rain water. By the walking together.
By the cloth deteriorating in the downpour.

The earth is where we are not.
They will condemn us for this.
But we will contain them.

The End of Travel

Voyage anxiety darkened the page, threatened the very trip.

But now, I'm back. And still, there's nothing. Nada. Surprisingly,
A relative ease in Nada.

God-like afternoons, the spokes of dreaming zip.

So the summer mounts the summer in reasonable
Ecstasies of heat.

Language as the ultimate lie-about, at least in its
Poetic sense, fashioning purposes out of no words in particular
Without once getting off its hairy back to look things up.

    A lazy Hermes
If such is possible, refusing space, disdaining worlds,
Eager only for the speed of thought, syntax undefinable.

Summer is repose, the season of the cat,
Time travel in its feline sense, the need for sleep
And the thread of slumber, a message delivered
In recollections of thunder, a message perhaps received,
Sun showers on the Mount of Olives, heat waves at Pere
Lachaise, etc.

To have etched the self more deeply
Plus some verbs, minus some verbs
On the interior and exterior of the glass.

A life whose austerities yield no song
But sonorities whose relation cannot be plumbed.

Crowd

A ruckus of forms swirls from the canvas of the street, as if the city itself were not really figurative, however much we are flecks of it, defining one anothers space.

It's all production and consumption, the eye included, one body going into another.

Let's call it an arch reality organized in such a way as to break you down, and truth be told, you are in complicity with it, milking aggression for all its worth.

But you can't be blamed for moving forward nonetheless, dispersed between the crevices of a desire without object, a fine perfume, if you like, pervading the corridors of each new tower complex to be traversed.

The state of arrest that holds all the molecules in rotation also makes us fly. But knowing what we know, fervor no longer transports.

Rather, black ponds of canvas engulf the head of the viewer.

I feel the same wave of depression every afternoon about 2, a phantom of panic attacking the pulse and then passing away, leaving me in its wake.

Does it really matter if I stand inside or outside the door?

Everything is connected here, a chaos of cells conspires, and at belly level the chords tie the beings in place.

Constitution

Over the city's bestudded darkness
Raptorial urgencies storm.
Reaches saturation point: a world
Exfoliates in the downpour, pedestrians
Clinging to doorways in heavy rain.
To the pornographic earth
Over which the run-off streams
As if it were the soul's pedestal,
Ignorance and inkling, beach and wave head
Readhere: to make the one frieze.
Was held in reverse: a deeper interpretation
Mockingly offered, the eventual acoustics
To make it all public. Life is a thwarting
of Logic, the culture voluminous, poverty stricken
But limpid. Well after the clouds stop coming
Our objection remains intact:
We are more than stories attached
To a birthplace. It's our epic side
Weathers things out.

Banned In Iran

I intuit the brilliance of the moon
in this room without windows or sense of time.

After all the most archaic unit is the moon
and language is lit with its reflected fire.

It isn't the moon I'm after,
it's barracudas at low tide circling the mirror.

It isn't the moon I'm after,
it's a single mother falling asleep next to her child

It isn't the moon I'm after,
it's a woman upbraiding the dawn's indifference

It isn't the moon I'm after,
its a mindful wraith, a rattling mystical June.

Room service, please send up six units of moon.
In solitude waking and dreaming are more easily one

As is impossible with others, unless you happen
to be in love or on the phone with the moon.

It isn't the moon I'm after:
what will not transform is the will to transform.

It isn't the moon I'm after:
rolling a carriage through hutongs in the rain.

It isn't the moon I'm after:
wild dogs, gypsies, desperate men

Camping out in the ruins of Byzantium's walls.
Inside the mosque I think about moons.

Low slung chandeliers and bowed believers
populate the interior of the moon room eclipsed.

Scatter moon dust over the menhir
if you can find moon dust and menhirs.

It isn't the moon I'm after,
its a peal of thunder and a rain of pearls

It isn't the moon I'm after,
its a great imam whose eyes ban idiocy

It isn't the moon I'm after,
its the ghost of a wolf haunting the Luberon

It isn't the moon I'm after,
its those wild dogs tearing up a crescent flag

It isn't the moon I'm after,
its the moon I'm after

Its the wound in the moon, the woo
in the moon, that womb in the moon

The screw in the moon, the spitting cobra
in the closet, the V imprint on the spitting cobra

It's the moon I'm after,
It's the moon I'm after, etc.

Family Romance Sonnet

She takes an early interest in the moon.
Thrusts her head back, a mimetic wolf.
From photographs, but where did she get the howl?
She is not yet Neolithic and I love her for it.
She sees more than the aesthetic I dash towards,
as a limestone quarry is always more than a quarry.
In the limestone I etch a vulva's lips, but only
to represent *you* as you were when you contracted.
All hypotheses unclench, every last one of them.
The alphabet is a net crammed with cuttlefish;
the crescent moon slips off another layer of clothes.
A special invitation, isn't it? One's
enough, there are never any guarantees.
The tide is pretty much everyone's mystery.

Fluid Situation

You and you and I from this will no way part.
Such is our inability to stack opinion,
to form any interpretation that might twist
away from ground, that ground-X our brains
must always grow, totally apart,
if a being is to cast its own form as origin.
Fact: certain walls no fist can drop.
Outlaw thoughts, sadly, get lost at last.
Thoughts, do you think? What ground?
Will we stay so unusually hinged to ourselves,
as when volcanic lava oozes forth
but is forced back under the crust?
Or will we finally join a visible pathway,
very timidly, thanks to some birth just now?
Swallowing everything in its tiny trickle,
a child aids identity across the rails of what must be.
A way to hold one's body, however small.
You and you and I who part from this
likely never found it.

Union

We I
ask of our orgasms

entry to ourselves

inside out
gathering of storms

to testify this flesh
is present.

The mind makes cubes of itself
and the eye opens up each cube,
discovers a woman inside in tight-fitting skins
Yes, a naked man worshipping Venus.

We I listen for the encroaching breeze

the mattress of days providing a stage
for clandestine public breathings

cries of delight from stoops
crowded with creation

Street noise as the groan of a manic God.

The broken world
must be broken again
into a fresh flow of sap,

Must add to its dissemination
with new clusters of form

we I in an impossible listening
for the architecture of orgasm

Now boarding the feathered ferry to take flight

Now crossing the other shore while staying put

Phallus is the death of the deathbed
down inside its room
Stiff, stiffer, stiffer

Mast-head leaving the testicled shore

Architecture not of rigor mortis but of
rigorous breath

To ask from love a trance of living, a lung of lust
to cross the other way by wing

Listening in the energies satin skin imparts

We I eating breakfast on a brilliant morning
above the city

In a brilliant light that someone had to make
and so we made it

Made it more than once
above the city

And I thought
this is very pretty to live like this

Let it always be spring
or summer

In spite of winter
things carry on

Events on the street, events
in the heart, bundled, bungled

But still beating

This morning I wake up
and then this

Outdoors,
the paroxysm.

Elations II

1

By what word to find our way?
Shiny boulder anchored in solitude.
Statues, lacerating rain,
lips as red as rowan-berries.
Such a male thing
to limn the woman's limbs,
drawing an orchestral sweep
around each movement
he's the one to shape.
Gorge caught in owls' hoot,
long drop down.
Wall I kicked, temple in tears.
Your tears of course; I cry less.
What did you say?
How did you say it?
Borne from the brine, the hot tub
of the sea, the mind *une meduse.*
To log myself into your light.
To form a diptych.
To believe in a screen.

2

The sky a boat
whose boatman squints back:
spire, swallow, sun.

Sparkle of distant snow.
Pitch black rock for miles around,
every inch of it younger than myself.
Test of vision: to see this crust
as thirsting skin.
Along a stream opened
to forms of song other than its own,
losing control of image's course.
Ancient power of fright and lust.
Must have been trying for many hours,
suddenly conscious of a large magpie.
Morning, no sleep, but at least morning.
A tigress, from insomnia conjured,
attests to the antique She;
woman, paw, bushy bee
slender as a curved sword,
drawn so near to death.

3

A finger rubbed against Creation:
what pertinent electrical storm?
Cliffs experienced as clarity, train tracks
drowned in cloud forest.
Please practice magic in me,
for I feel overwhelmed by what
I lusted for, who came
jealous of language,
devoid of all human dress.
Canal driven, camel drawn,
restless creature glass-trapped,

coming on the glass.
Moving dunes impossible to map.
Motherland, desert poplars:
ripest fruit well out of reach.
Are they cops? What gold chain?
Unspoken words block the raid.
Shiny boulder anchored in solitude.
Mass quivering with thought
beached jellyfish even looks like brain.

4

Things inanimate and without life
remain inanimate and without life:
great abundance of hair,
thick, black, rolling.
A golden crow
living only on special apples.
Missing gas pump,
roadmarker you don't remember passing,
a yearning to linger, to loll far far
longer, avoid the grass next door
whose populace shore
fakes such moving cradle.
Cave goats with whom
a monk runs naked, assuming
the cave's dimness conceals his shame;
suddenly, enlightenment strikes.
Heavenly Mountain in a snowstorm:
camels and goats block the road, their gazes
red beams in the headlights, Kazaks on horseback
herding animals towards even higher grazing.

5

Casting about hungrily
for light to build on,
fantasizing stony landscape
our possible shrine.
Aphrodite trapezes over objecthood,
the somber sky its backdrop in us,
never firm. Watching a crater bird bank
and rise, steam vomiting to all sides.
Wrestling in the flower, to form
a diptych. Unchiseled boulders
joined perfectly at each edge:
nimblest objects inured to age,
each stone speaking to the others.
Hadrian's Wall, Wailing Wall,
Great Wall: Inca Roca tops them all.
So MOMA makes itself over, sculpture garden
sculptures gone, the whole garden shuttered.
Here, this long blue poignant jellyfish tentacle
doubles as his spine.
— America's brightest source.

6

Super intelligent tiger loose near
Mt. Rainier, the local game warden
reading it Rilke, hoping
to draw the beast into the clearing.
I was peeking into the alley

where women show their thighs
when it dawned on me: I was asleep.
An arcade atmosphere, lurid,
illicit, late at night.
Later that morning the best available hounds
tree the tiger; before any trackers arrive
the cat transforms into a crow, flutters off.
The lioness allows her lids to droop.
Her tail scoots away the flies.
Of a single great revolving goal
we only get guerrilla glimpses.
As the mind makes loopdieloops:
scarves, eyes, long shapely legs.
Lips as red as berries pleading for their name.
The dreamer is always distant.

7

So going around consciousness.
If it weren't for crippling sexual desire
I would never go, never get.
Longing to seize some hinge essentially unseizable.
Tangerines in a bowl, olfactory anticipation.
Every stone is talking to every other,
as per America's dream.
Climbing the hairpin coast
out from town, surviving each curve
to round higher, into the headlands.
To remain in the turbulence
one's mind adrift, working the waves.
It dawned on me this was the law

or logos, the law or pathos, the law
or a fine wine spilling on the floor.
I walk among olive groves, I meditate on
Manhattan's fabled energy, favored cliches.
Volcanic eruption, tiny trickle, lava
oozing from a dark, distant mound.
Loss piled on loss: sensory find, sensory find.

8

Condors line the last tree's limbs.
Nearly midnight in the cold highlands.
Barking of a dog beyond any conceptual framework.
Mind never quite freed from brine's first foaming.
Powerful forces bind beings together,
bending our shapes, spatter after spatter.
"Tongue" is a word, so is "tip."
Anticipating elation, ever alert.
Enameled dolmen anchoring the plane,
Europeans medivaced out of the gorge.
I'll manage without certain of their curlicues
if that's what it takes, I mean tone down
certain tendencies, tune out some sirens,
those that I can. Mind spawns
minds spawns mind spasms.
Cherished work, probable earth, mutest shell.
Who season after season adds something to the brew.
Always only wanted those grapes, still cool,
on a plate in the afternoon sun. OK then.
Grapes on a plate: afternoon sun. Cool.

The Sun Bittern

The man craved the animal
and his own humanity, dipped
his paddle into the stream and held it there,
just poised, as the sun bittern thrashed
its wings and flew away in a huff
horizontal to the water, tail feathers churning.
Just one part of the life of a stream
whose god had never been named
or the memory of whose name
had not been preserved. The man craved
humidity, the way air preserved water
postponing for hours the moment of release.
Each rustle left an imprint, each basilisk mattered.
Sharks rushed upstream after fresh water fish
it hardly seemed possible.
And his humanity was deepened
seeing how the jaguar had left prints
would be washed away by the next morning's tide.

The man's humanity had been deepened;
but *humanitas* is the order that cancels other worlds.
Initiation into other orders, where initiate
would mean simply to be there, not who one was,
would never be possible. They were too much
apart. He was more dangerous than ever.
Only if the forest's god, the stream's deity,
had received its new name could the circle be complete.
For that to happen he would have to become a polytheist.
Which he did. (Try out various names in your mouth.)

Point of Entry II

Feeling comes to respect
  some outward form,
evolving kinship
  between word and event,
sensation and mimetic gesture
  wriggling to reach
some meeting point
          imagined.

To respect this relation,
a coming-into-itself as real,
  being-in and being-for
having walked the aisle that leads
  to exile's end.
A stake in the world
after it's been transfigured
  by a magic "no,"
before creation, after creation
or rather, as it happens,
  both pure and full.

How limited the time
  one realizes
to be one's time. In which
one fills moments with a serious making,
  momentous.
(I'd lanced a certain skepticism
  some weeks back
without even being aware.)

Life that leads by pointing,
the way an infant, still mute,
    manages to point.
Mango. Fish plate. Black lab pup
dabbing his paw in ocean foam.
The words held in reserve
    aren't any more reserved,
the world glows red.
That dog swimming out
   a bit among the waves.
Grapefruit. Flower. Flock of ibis
   taking flight.

Like being on an airplane
and suddenly realizing
you don't care if you ever arrive:
    you love so intently
the point to which you are moving
    your present
becomes infused by it
and even at this distance
 you cannot be distracted
     or denied.

Freed from impatience,
    to find one's time.
Music as fits your mood.

A coming-into-itself
      as real,
a fact achieved
     where there can be no facts,

only feeling,
    phosphorescent.

What you clasp
      is what
you are,
who grasps you,
      is you.
As real as any apparition.
A kinship among coordinates
which name each other King.

Disorder Sonnet

Left to its nuns the soul is literary,
nouns loaded onto provided transportation.
Yet it's the unbundled traveler
that goes further into beauty,
her *voudon* that makes elegance from meat.
A light so nude it disorients dunes.
Spill of our forms, foam
and thunderstorm that shudders
in almost delighted loins,
O tolerant sieve that daily flaunts
its latency over incoherence, nightflower.
An exile its never forced.
The svelte caravan advances in glorious disarray.
Left to its verbs the soul is always fervent.

IV

The New Babel

o

Babel of course is the fall of a Tower, followed by a vast, manipulated confusion of words.

Babble is language's beginning, before it's a language, while it's still song.

As Babel is both a ground and a zero, Middle English *grund* and Arabic *zefir, cipher,* Gallacized *zero* — let's call it Ground Zero.

Babel is defiance of the demiurge and hubris of the heart, ziggurat aimed at suns yet unborn, inside the mouth the mouth as desire: man creates gods.

Where before stood the North and the South now yawns a smoldering Cleft, smoke subject to variable breezes.

The smoke contains bodies; we breathe one another. Thus, Babel is Kabul. We breathe one another.

As Ares broods over all the world's capitals: fragments of furniture spun from seized cockpits, strangers blinking into craters of Mars.

Babel is Kabul: Babel's a Bible in a motel room dresser in Birmingham, Alabama: Babel's the Battery Park Esplanade and the people still waiting in the airport in Santo Domingo.

Babel: the most beautiful girl in all of Kashgar, black haired, black eyed, maybe 13 years old, in a gay red dress, gazing admiringly at the foreign lady chance brought to her alley, gently, tentatively, mouthing a single phrase in English, addressed to that lady: "How do you do?"

Babel is mettlesome, its scrotum melted some, our mad extravagant metropolis, not bashful, still seeking the heights.

Babel was Mesopotamia, its era's only superpower: redound of Gilgamesh, modern day Iraq.

Babel is Baghdad, Babel is Belgrade, Babel's our backyard, a World that incessantly trades names with itself.

Babble in three languages, babble in three thousand: put on a bib.

A baby babbled of lions eating books. And those lions ate books: Babel is books on the shelves of the Bibliotheque Queer.

No rabble in Babel: everyone's speech an equally valid muse. Thus: bomb them with butter.

Here is the blade with which Babel's abolished, here are the furrows where Babel begins, which no seed can boycott.

Babel rinses its parents in sorrow, Babel rewards its makers with slowworms, Babel is birth, rebuilding with cranes all sorts of crimes, the way life is a dagger, the way all wars begin with some bed's disaster.

Who shaved her cunt with Babel's boxcutter: born from the rubble, "ba" is for father, "ma" is for mother, sacred baboons patrolling her precincts.

Babel is Buddha dispensing with words, Babel is mating, thunder, whale blubber and rain, Babel is blame, Babel is ax, Babel is Bush-ben-Laden and fame.

As tall facades crumble like rockface, so many unbound mountains, Captain FBI simply offers "My bad."

Babble of waves, babble of wharves, of merchants and stores, city proud of its iron and brains: babble is braggart, babble is pulpit, babble's a word on the tip of your tongue or the trouble stored in a bull's flaring nostrils.

I'm down with the Tower of Babel.

I can't even enjoy a blade of grass unless I know there's a subway handy or record store or some other sign that people do not totally regret life.

Is stumble, is stutter, is stone smooth as skin, towers swaying the way they sway in the wind, as a person is always his tongue's own half-witting puppet.

Is the baker whose bagels are too hot, whose pancakes are unscaleable, whose loaves are uncanny and sprinkled with pain.

Is flesh covered with brine, is bitumen cracked with fever, wolves in the blood howling to the gibbous heart.

Babel is the beaten ballplayer who goes ballistic; Babel is an icicle in your mouth as melodious as a flute, as percussive in its dripping as drums.

Tower whose twisted tendrils resemble trellis and grapes, destruction demanded by the Dionysus of east meeting west, an unwillingness to consent to any loss of the self.

Babel is nothing but the celebration of words, talk armed with torches, dreams capsized by bigger dreams, the truth of each crater, the "bang bang" that wakes one from dream, the gap between "it's an accident" and "my god it's intentional," the B1 Bomber they're building and building, the backlash and the backlash to backlash and the backlash to backlash to backlash, O Barrio of Barriers, *our* republic of fear.

Enough elasticity to move with the wind, enough stiffness so that people can't know the building is moving: Babel is bubble gum stuck to your face.

Babel is presence, Babel is absence: nothing but the celebration of presence. *No mas* to sacred explosions, *no mas* to the occupation of land: sacred explosions, the occupation of land.

Babel is how a man howls as he leaps from the heights, where no other man can hear him; Babel is that moment of imagining one can fly, a brevity that lasts forever in Babel's unconscious.

Babel is a ray of sunlight crashing earthbound, a rivulet of rays crashing earthbound, a field mined with light.

The Tower of Babel: word up.

If architecture is frozen music, then these melted, smoking shards are its melodies, its incandescent burial grounds — Babel become what begs you to sing it.

I

" . . . it is precisely in the heat of the war that those deep social convulsions take place that destroy old institutions and remold man, that, in other words, the seeds of peace germinate in the devastation's of war. Man's intense longing for peace is never so strong as it is at a time of war. Hence, in no other social circumstance are there so many strong impulses intent on changing the conditions that produce war. Man learned to construct dams when he suffered from floods. Peace can be hammered out only at a time of war, then and only then." — Wilhelm Reich, *The Mass Psychology of Fascism*

How many waves has the moon generated in the Persian Gulf since 1991?

How many waves have the moon and the Atlantic collaborated on since 1491-and-a-half?

What was the total number of breakers to have risen from the earth's seas before life ever began?

Can one figure the number of waves the Pacific has wept since Nagasaki and Hiroshima?

They hang flags the way horses wear blinders; they hang flags in great abundance. They want wars, without realizing it.

They signal war, some realizing it and some without realizing it; they wave flags the way matadors wave red.

Each suffering silently in the silence of his, her, or its own bed; two faucets dripping out of sync; three sinks, four sinks, five sinks, each with a dripping faucet; all the seas whipped and tossed by colossal winds.

The Tower of Babel: landlocked, an abandoned worksite farmers come to quarry.

The Tower of Babel: in the text it's preceded by a Flood.

Inside a New Mexican waterfall comes more than water, more than gravity, less than anything this moment's coarsening could ever put in words.

It's natural for water to fall. It's natural for water to fall from cliffs and it's natural for towers to melt when exposed to overwhelming heat. This applies equally to shacks. October 7th, 2001.

Mud huts have their own way of falling, of being destructively transformed. October 8th, 2001.

The death of peace happened long ago but went unmarked by any stone or number.

The wars come in waves.

Collateral damage is a literary term but the text's main force falls on the text's opponent.

Poetry: death without peace.

August 6th, 1945: unending death.

Dying each death. Refusing to kill. October 11th, 2001.

October 12th, 2001: No, those are my tax dollars.

As even grief gives way to its own self-indulgence. Bush's address to the Nation, September 20th, 2001.

The Nation wallows in its own grief, the Nation's mistakes are glorified, laureled, transformed into heroic moments, sacrificial acts: acts that would have been unnecessary if earlier mistakes had been avoided higher up, among the elites; and indeed it may be said those who died sacrificed themselves for the oil elites' sins. Fall, 2001.

Neither innocent, nor deserving of the force of those flames: no one deserves the force of those flames, no one is innocent.

Grief. Just grief. Unadorned by heroic gesture, deprived of that heroic consolation the bereaved are presumed to need. But do the bereaved really need to see their dead as heroic? Or do the bereaved need to see their dead loves as those cheated of their lives by a gratuitous dialectic of disproportionate extremes?

Some other kind of gesture: some other kind of mission: some other kind of interior life.

Not the fireman who brought his siren to the Times Square Peace Rally, drowning each speech, each speaker, in the blare of his profession: but the firemen and the women digging in the mass grave they were the first to declare a sacred ground.

Inside a New Mexican waterfall comes more than water, more than gravity, more than fatal plunge, something subtlely less than a monotheist could ever put in words.

The waves the Pacific has wept since Nagasaki and Hiroshima continually multiply.

It's natural for water to fall. It's natural to imagine the end of the world. In imagining the end of the world we protect our way of life.

In those days in which answers are offered as self-evident, hammer out a new tower of Babel: not confusion but words as the impulse to transmute the silence of dumb agreement, no longer numb before a single divine authority or empire.

Let a new tower of Babel touch the sky. Let a new tower of Babel bend responsively to the moon. Ishtar, Inshallah, Quetzlcoatl. Babble babble babble.

2

Barry Bearak, *The New York Times*, December 15th, 2001, Madoo, Afghanistan:

" Perhaps someday there will be a reckoning for this tiny village of 15 houses, all of them obliterated into splintered wood and dust by American bombs. United States military officials might explain why 55 people died here on December 1st . . . But more likely, Madoo will not learn whether the bombs fell by mistake or on purpose, and the matter will be forgotten amid the larger consequences of war. It is left an anonymous hamlet with anonymous people buried in anonymous graves . . . America's own anti-Taliban allies were horrified, claiming the targeting had been mistaken and that hundreds of innocents had been killed. It was 'like a crime against humanity', said Hajji Muhammad Zaman, a military commander in the region."

Madoo's farmers are people in pieces. They've become their own fertilizer . . . assuming the rains come we did them a favor, suggests a cartoon version of Secretary of Defense R. (Big laugh). But really there is no need for such a cartoon. We've already firmly established the concept of collateral damages.

He who sees with his heart, as Paz would have it, sees Madoo as himself; and who can't see Madoo with his heart? ("Men with fossil minds, with oily tongues" suggests the cartoonist.)

Every face, a mask; every house a ruin of mudbrick and wood.

Whose sisters were killed? Collateral Damage can't ever say beforehand. (Terrorists don't target specific sisters.) (The American attack came in four separate waves.)

After Madoo, to write poetry is barbaric. (Theodor Adorno).

"'We've yet to find their bodies'"
"'many layers to this rubble'"
"'and now we live with this'"
"'mystery'":

Sayeth the elder Mr. Gul, Madoo resident,
though he might be speaking of Manhattan.

"Sorrowful old man" "white beard" "furrowed forehead":

"then Paia Gul" "young man" "bitter eyed": "' I blame'"
"'the Arabs'" "'then amended his own'" "'statement'"

"' I blame the Arabs'" "'and the Americans'"
"'They are all terrible people'"
"'they are all the worst in the world'"
"'most of the dead were children.'"

Fragrance bird song wheatfields
Mr. Bearak reporting two weeks after Madoo's apocalypse.
Harvesting scrap metal from bombs,
hopes of surviving winter.

Beyond anecdote sounds a hymn we can only hum, humble in
our making,
the birds scribbling like authors in a startling ephemera of air.

"Walking in the vegetable patch
late at night, I was startled to find
the severed head of my
daughter lying on the ground.

Her eyes were upturned, gazing at me, ecstatic-like . . .

(From a distance it appeared
to be a stone, hallooed with light,
as if cast there by the Big Bang.)

What on earth are you doing, I said,
you look ridiculous.

Some boys buried me here,
she said sullenly."
— Araki Yasusada, *Doubled Flowering,* the foothills
surrounding Hiroshima, December 25th, 1945

Craters. Tractor carcass. Dead sheep.
   Urn crushed to disc;
unendurable, "unintended," un-American
    Ax Americana;
far from Mecca, in Madoo, Tora Bora,
 one undamaged room.

Anger cannot be buried.

Prayer is perfect when he who prays remembers not that he is praying.

Everything dead trembles.(Kandinsky)

Note: E-Mail the reporter, ask if there were ever rows of poplars.

Moonstone sucked into the atmosphere of dwarfed arts; no Hero but also no Nero; the half that faces us is full tonight.

As the Kaushitaki Upanishad has it, "the breath of life is one."

The word "Madoo" is a transcription of a Pashtun name the reporter must have sounded out.

In English, then, "Madoo."

In English the name "Madoo" derives from an old Scottish word meaning "my dove."

3

He imagined himself the famous wise man who'd succeeded in speaking with desert sand.

Not so wise of him to make the very sand in which he wandered quite so famed.

How wise was it for this well dressed man surrounded by silence to continue to babble when no one was there?

There was plenty of air. All of it was very hot.

Twenty-one steps into the desert and the road disappears from view. Any sense of direction departs one's brain like a hummingbird. No one would know where you'd gone, nor would you.

The dunes are moving. The road disappears even if you remain motionless, planted in its middle. One might hire people to sweep the sand. But that takes money.

The silence of the Taklimakan is much renowned.

The Chinese built the road for oil trucks. To barrel through. And they do. Though it hardly matters. Trucks are little dots.

He imagined himself the obscure wise man who'd learned to speak with desert poplars.

"How do you live in a desert?" he asked an especially sturdy tree, and waited. For "truth" comes from "tree."

In a startling ephemera of air pinkness swirls from the goodbye sun, energy lifts from under its skirt, or perhaps it's the man, its the man turning lavender with love.

And the desert poplar answered: " put on a bib." Then added: "Please allow the word 'calm.'"

And the man went away, not sure he'd understood, not sure he'd ever spoken the tongue of desert poplars.

But he put on a bib. He wore the bib always. In the bedroom. In the boardroom.

When the other executives asked him what was happening he answered calmly: "I remain a kid."

The mind's future is never given.

Of course the wise man was eventually sacked.

The road had disappeared from beneath his legs.

Sand irritates the first sentinels.

My vocabulary did this to me, he thought.

I'll have to increase my vocabulary.

4

To begin to build the New Babel where the Old Babel had previously stood.

Babel is water freezing, despite the blinding sun, above a storefront grating on Broadway and 168th; Babel's an icicle that wants you to come over and stroke it through your warm leather glove.

To rebuild lower Manhattan, as Hiroshima was rebuilt, however comparatively small the scale of this new destruction, cormorants drying their wings in a warm stream of air.

"*Kom,* beside near, by with. Germanic *ga,* Old English *ge,* together. Latin *cum,* come with. Suffixed form *kom-tra,* in Latin *contra,* against, suffixed form *kom-yo,* in Greek *koinos,* common shared."

Thus: it's come time to come, it's past time to come against (patriotism as bobbled libido).

Babel is the only acceptable weapon, a tongue in your mouth, then someone else's tongue in your mouth; a tongue in the mouth is the only acceptable weapon and here comes someone else's tongue.

Babel is never, ever commodity; Babel is never ever ever commodity, since commodity fells it.

Liberate desire from commodity, though lingerie is desirable; Babel is contradiction without being hypocritical, commodity enticing care.

Babel is hands on shoulders, caresses for the breasts, uninterrupted burning apple wood, uninterrupted shining cherry wood, mists sprung from inner sinews and moistening lips.

How rhyme the whole of a redwood? That's the flower Babel has growing in its brain.

Babel's a belly as flat as a book, a curve as gentle as a dune, a dream as supple as a gymnast.

A cock edging into your mouth, a pussy encircling your middle finger: babble's home.

Babel is the desire to affirm when you know it's not possible, a bulge in your pants as soft as the rock a petroglyph maker carves into; Babel's a nose unconventionally long that nonetheless turns you on, a twist in the argument that leaves you suddenly speechless, the Biblical prophets when they fall back in awe, tunnels of the cranium no spark has ever flown down before, learning not only to wield the great wheel but also to yield to it.

Babel's a snow leopard whose presence commands silence, a tiger you transform into the moment your lids are lowered, a dog with his nose up another dog's ass; Babel's a clean hyena and a dirty hyena, a clean hyena and a drooling hyena, a clean hyena and a meercat with an awfully pointy head.

Babel's the bubble always bursting, the banks going bankrupt, the form of pleasure that costs you nothing but your own energy as you generate it.

Babel's a series of caresses that pass one into another.

Babel involves taking it upon yourself to stand, head bared, beneath the tempests of the Lord, in order to seize the Father's lightning with your hands, and offer the people this gift of Heaven, veiled in your song. (Hölderlin).

As I am ready to honor you and to blaspheme against you at one and the same time, my mind the mosque in which man and woman mingle — Mr. Last Monotheistic God Still Standing.

Babel is consciousness and comsciousness, cocksciousness and cuntsciousness, and comsciousness and consciousness taste here, and here, and here . . .

Working hypothesis #1: a precise for love and not precision bombing.

5

Nerves shrouded beneath the burka, as prescribed in certain countries; one's eye encountering only the burka, as experienced in certain cultures: whole realms in which men require one another to live behind the burka.

Not the techno-veil of consumer culture but the techno-burka, without any hole for the head.

It is a savage sensibility, savage and delicate, scored by superabundance and need, scandalized and desensitized by its own hunger for violence. Its adolescents shoot up their own schools, their own peers, then commit suicide. Their culture is a death-mask, the burka its insignia, hooded hordes saturated in a thuglike, thinglike cult of senseless hurt, spawned by the most sophisticated marketeers.

The interior burka which impedes apperception, the heavy burka that goes with me, the opaque burka whose presence mocks reflection, the mandatory burka worn in the body politic, the bottled burka concealing the body from the erotic self, the bad opposition of burka and bikini, and other strange customs practiced there: to pretend power is not rooted in sexual urgency, to shift the burden of such urgency onto children unprepared to bare it.

Self-inflicted concealment always falls to self-reflection's raid, or so the Enlightenment taught and founding fathers bathed; "the eye that avoids seeing, sickens."

No Orientalism, no exoticism, no dehumanization of the other: our citizens refuse to any longer wear the black or turquoise burka.

No refuge in victimhood, in uniform amnesia, in hooded subjectivity: Americans will no longer throw a burlap sack over events that happen elsewhere in the world, will no longer squint at the world from behind their security burka.

No nationalism that blinds one to the terrible crimes of the Nation: the Attorney General will no longer throw the burka over the crimes he himself perpetrates, nor will the Secretary of Defense.

No false modesty, no passing on the buck: the Presidency and other machines of capital are no longer concealed by their various and sundry burkas.

Papers fluttering from the Tower of Babel's burning windows indicate that words are all that's left; paper survives where flesh and beams are shattered. Thus Babel is never burka and humans must honor bones with words.

Babel survives the revelation of its own mystery, as do women; the burka is nothing but its own formless bulk.

Burka is the triumph of the masculine over the feminine, banishing the feminine from public life, as words are banished from public life in a culture in which the reality of words are hidden.

Babel is the masculine that strives to reach the feminine and always fails, in falling back begins to live itself in all its seed potential.

Babel is the feminine ambition and potentiality of all things, inclusive of those specialized cells that strive for verticality.

If one could seize the dead stars and gather all those stones in one place in order to construct a tower . . .

And yet the body floats in a placenta of words and no word is ever comprehensible except as it emerges quivering from between the legs, naked as the space between the legs, and, in the next twinkle, comes howling, soon to fall back again, no more but no less than the words it has quickly scattered . . .

It's the little pin that pricks the giant balloon (Oppen). It's the sperm racing for the egg. A firing that has nothing to do with missiles.

Working hypothesis #2: a precise for love and not a precision bombing.

6

bobble libido brain Pentagon seclusion

village Allah songbirds sisters lavender

mystery metal Emir American icicle

children daisy plumes mudbrick phallus

sheep quetzlcoatl airport Orphic President

bib life-fire farmer feminine vegetable patch

moonstone Mecca Manhattan Pashtun apperception

moonstone Mother poplar dam prayer

Ax E-Mail hallooed daughter downtown

kiss Oriental precision grief Scottish.

7

What's worshipped isn't upstairs. You've kissed it often beside the sweet flanks of living oak, which is why you know it to be peripherally, pictured and unpictured thought, a wet rush between the legs, a bond between contingent realities and Babylon's tower, for which will yet come a fitting word.

The flowerpots break around you, the tortoise shells lose their markings, at that moment when the city seems to come unbound. Like the Cultural Revolution all over again, the Fathers sent to the countryside, the break with the Mother final, Central Park stretching outwards like a vast, slow-motion expanse, scattered with bystanders frozen in their disbelief. You knew your skin would forever hunger, that tears and their accompaniment would always sound out the absence of words; Big Character Posters would be the business of the day, that, and rousting dens of tigers. By December green water collects in the crater pit.

Yet "the deeper unsatisfied war beneath and behind the declared war"(Duncan), the conflicting egotism's, the hooligans of hubris, combat groups, policies of chaos, and petroleum spread, all are bound in a larger dialectic sensation momentarily shatters. Abundance explodes around you, the bounty hurtles past, and is even more wrenching for its beauty: boulders and blinding sun.

And the tongues were so baffled that each became scatterbrain to his friend, until not even the husband and the wife any longer knew how to speak with each other . . . murderers hard at work above ground, and all you have are these perceptions organized in little packets of dynamic resolve, memory and anticipation making reciprocal stands, having by now long since accepted the most difficult brain assignment our tribe can ever be charged with. Dazzling.

Sand irritates the first sentinels.

"Save those who weep"(Eluard).

What's worshipped isn't upstairs. Because this is already the uppermost floor. As Bina, in Bengali, refers to the instrument that Saraswati, goddess of learning, was destined to strum. Feel the tautness of those strings. Remember the books with torn covers and cover pages and thus no titles and authors: words read in their purest form, books acquired on the sly, *a fire finally acknowledged as impossible to put out.*

What's worshipped isn't upstairs. Because this is the ground floor. Among mysterious plants you bask in someone who's your sun yet rests beneath you, like a foundation. Run your fingers between her toes. Cracks of a source that holds marvel on marvel.

Things do assemble in their own rotunda; a wood stork hunches in the cypress, part of a greater ecosystem, without any particular capital or center.

The hour really is getting younger.

Designed by
Samuel Retsov

Text: 12 pt Centaur

acid-free paper

Printed by
McNaughton & Gunn